Starting Life

Butterfly

Claire Llewellyn
illustrated by Simon Mendez

It is a warm summer afternoon, and a monarch butterfly is laying her eggs. She lays them on a milkweed plant—one egg to each juicy leaf.

Monarchs always lay their eggs on milkweed plants so the young can feed on the leaves.

Milkweed plant

Monarch butterfly

A female flies away after laying her eggs. She does not stay and care for her young.

A butterfly's eggs have hard shells covered with tiny ridges. They protect the creature that is growing inside until it hatches.

Red milkweed beetle

Egg

A female monarch lays about 400 eggs in all. They are safely stuc̶ hidden ben̶

3

Four days later the eggs hatch into caterpillars. The tiny creatures are very hungry. First, they eat their egg shells, then they feed on the plant.

The eggs change from white to brown when they are ready to hatch.

Newly-hatched caterpillars are very tiny. They have black heads and pale bodies.

Monarch caterpillar

Milkweed contains a poison. It does not hurt monarch caterpillars, but it makes them taste very bad so that predators will leave them alone!

Tachinid fly

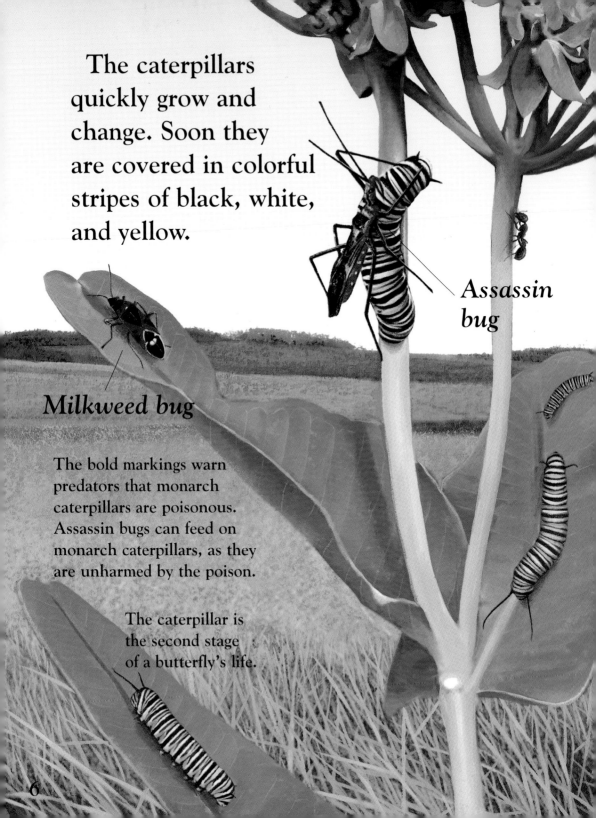

The caterpillars quickly grow and change. Soon they are covered in colorful stripes of black, white, and yellow.

Assassin bug

Milkweed bug

The bold markings warn predators that monarch caterpillars are poisonous. Assassin bugs can feed on monarch caterpillars, as they are unharmed by the poison.

The caterpillar is the second stage of a butterfly's life.

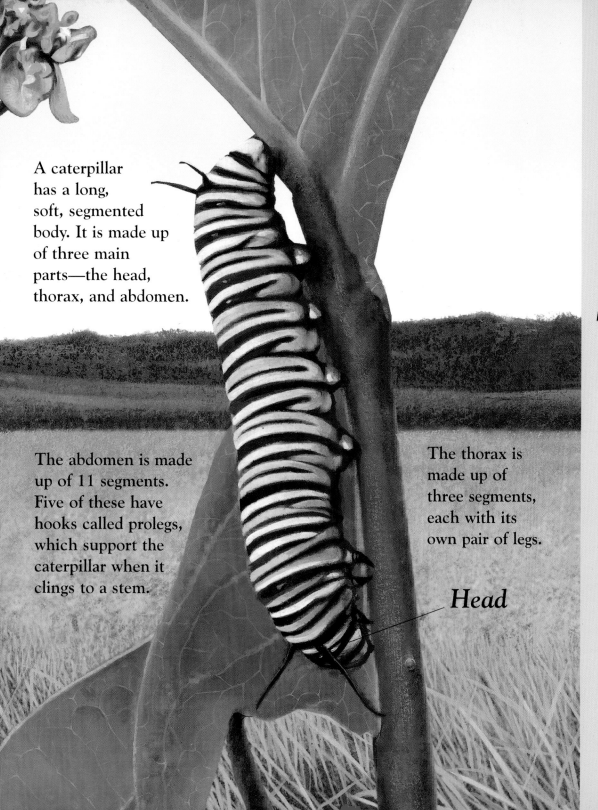

A caterpillar has a long, soft, segmented body. It is made up of three main parts—the head, thorax, and abdomen.

The abdomen is made up of 11 segments. Five of these have hooks called prolegs, which support the caterpillar when it clings to a stem.

The thorax is made up of three segments, each with its own pair of legs.

Head

Munch, munch, munch—a caterpillar never stops eating, leaf after leaf after leaf. All that food makes it grow very quickly, so that soon its skin feels tight.

Milkweed plants are very tall and have plenty of juicy leaves.

Caterpillars hardly have to move to feed. They strip one leaf, then crawl on to another.

Some wasps lay their eggs on a caterpillar's body. The eggs hatch into tiny grubs that feed on the caterpillar and kill it.

Braconid wasp

One day—pop! Its skin bursts open. Underneath there is a soft new skin in a larger size. Caterpillars can only grow by shedding their skins—they do it five times in all.

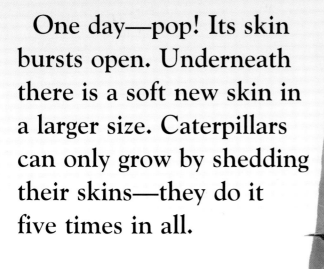

A caterpillar grows at an amazing rate. After two weeks it is 50 times bigger than when it hatched from the egg.

When a caterpillar has wriggled out of its old skin it has a brand new skin with plenty of room to grow. The old skin contains a lot of nutrition, so the caterpillar eats it up.

9

After two weeks, the caterpillar is full-grown. It stops feeding, spins a soft silk pad, and hangs upside-down. Its striped skin splits open for the very last time.

Caterpillar

Stage 1
The caterpillar is ready to change into a chrysalis. It fastens itself to a stem and hangs down in the shape of a J.

Fire ant

Stage 4
The chrysalis hardens and turns a dark, metallic color.

Now the caterpillar looks very different. It has changed into a hard case called a chrysalis. The chrysalis does not move or feed, but it is very much alive!

Stage 3
The new chrysalis is milky-green and very soft.

New chrysalis

Stage 2
The caterpillar sheds its skin one last time. Underneath the old skin, the chrysalis can be seen.

For two weeks, the chrysalis hangs from the stem. Most of the time it is very still, but now and then it suddenly twitches. Inside, huge changes are taking place. Soon, bright colors—black, white, and a fiery orange—can be seen through the chrysalis walls.

A butterfly takes about two weeks to develop inside the chrysalis. Then it is ready to make its way out.

One day the dry case splits open, and a new creature struggles out. It is a monarch butterfly! The monarch has been through many changes.

Empty chrysalis

This special way of growing and changing is called metamorphosis.

The butterfly struggles out of the chrysalis. Its wings are damp and crumpled, and it is very tired.

The butterfly unfolds its wings so that they dry in the sun.

The new butterfly has a delicate body with three pairs of legs and three parts to its body—the head, thorax, and abdomen. It has four colorful wings that are covered with shimmering scales.

Butterflies have huge eyes called compound eyes, made up of thousands of tiny lenses.

Male monarch butterfly

It's easy to tell male and female monarchs apart. The males have a black spot on each back wing. The females do not.

A monarch butterfly has two pairs of wings. They measure 4 inches (10 cm) from tip to tip, which is roughly the width of your hand.

Butterflies belong to a group of animals called insects. All insects have three parts to their body and three pairs of legs.

On its head, the butterfly has two long antennae that pick up smells and movements in the air. It has two large eyes, packed with tiny lenses, that help it to see all around.

Female monarch butterfly

The butterfly has six legs, each tipped with tiny claws so it can cling to flowers and stems.

Butterflies are adults. They do not need food for growing. They need it to repair their bodies and fuel them for flight.

Butterflies feed on nectar, the sugar-sweet juice inside every flower. They see the flowers as they fly through the air, then land and use taste sensors on their feet to find the pool of nectar. Now they uncurl their straw-like tongues, and suck up the nectar.

Nectar smells as sweet as honey. Butterflies pick up its scent in the air using their antennae.

Mullein

The milkweed withers by late summer, so the monarchs feed on other flowers, such as mullein and blazing star. They begin to lose their precious protection because, without milkweed, they don't taste quite so bad!

In early summer, monarchs feed on milkweed flowers. The poison in these plants protects the monarchs by giving them a bitter taste.

Crab spider

Blazing star

The butterfly feeds through a tube called the proboscis, which is hollow like a drinking straw. The proboscis curls away when it is not in use.

Monarch butterflies lay eggs all summer long. Each week new eggs hatch into caterpillars, and new butterflies fly into the air. As the cooler days of autumn approach, the older butterflies die. But the newer ones leave on a long journey called migration and travel to warmer lands.

Monarchs fly in huge masses over cities, forests, mountains, and deserts on their way to their winter roosts.

The butterflies travel on warm, sunny days, moving southwest towards California or Mexico.

Monarch butterflies fly south in the autumn, travelling up to 3,000 miles (4,800 km) to Mexico and California. New monarchs make the trip each year. No butterfly ever does it twice. So how do the butterflies find their way? And how can they travel so far? Scientists still do not know the answers.

Monarchs are experts at riding the wind. On some days they travel up to 124 miles (200 km).

The butterflies spend the winter months sheltering in mountain forests. The monarchs roost together like birds, clinging to the trunks and branches of the trees. As millions of them huddle tightly together, they sink into a winter sleep, which is known as hibernation.

The monarchs roost in fir trees, gripping the bark and needles with tiny claws on their feet.

Gray catbird

A black-eared mouse drags a monarch back to its burrow to feed to its young.

But even as they hibernate, the butterflies are in danger. The poison in their bodies that used to protect them has almost disappeared. Now they make a welcome feast for the hungry forest birds and mice that come to eat their fill.

The butterflies in the middle of a roost are warmer than those outside. They are also safer from mice or birds.

Brown-headed cowbird

Monarch butterflies roost together in huge groups called colonies. Each colony contains a million or more.

Many birds feed on the hibernating monarchs. Some birds eat only the abdomen, and avoid the still-poisonous wings.

Black-headed grosbeak

After five cold months, spring returns to the forest. The days are growing longer and brighter, and the monarchs begin to stir. Soon millions of butterflies take to the air and, in a dazzling flurry of shimmering wings, the males and females mate.

In early April, the females seek out milkweed plants and begin to lay their eggs.

The butterflies feed on spring flowers to fuel themselves for their journey north.

Female monarch

New eggs

Now all the butterflies leave the forest, and fly north to cooler lands. Again and again, they halt their flight to feed on sweet-smelling flowers. Soon, one of the females sees a milkweed plant. As she lands and lays her first egg, a new butterfly's life begins.

Milkweed plants grow in many different places. As long as there are milkweeds, there will always be plenty of monarchs!

Male monarch

Glossary and Index